THE ART OF THE RENAISSANCE

Nathaniel Harris

A Compilation of Works from the
BRIDGEMAN ART LIBRARY

SIENA

Renaissance

This edition first published in 1995 by
Parragon Book Service Ltd
Units 13-17 Avonbridge Industrial Estate
Atlantic Road
Avonmouth
Bristol BS11 9QD

ISBN 0 75250 736 2

Printed in Italy

Editors: Barbara Horn, Alexa Stace, Alison Stace, Tucker Slingsby Ltd and Jennifer Warner.
Designers: Robert Mathias and Helen Mathias
Picture Research: Kathy Lockley

The publishers would like to thank Joanna Hartley at the Bridgeman Art Library for her invaluable help.

THE RENAISSANCE is one of the most familiar episodes in the history of art, and almost everybody has heard of great masters such as Leonardo da Vinci and Michelangelo. The Renaissance was mainly centred on 15th and 16th-century Italy, although the Italians learned much from foreign artists, and eventually 'exported' their styles and techniques to create a 'Northern Renaissance'.

The essential Italian achievement was to create an art based on observing, faithfully reproducing, and celebrating the world of man and nature. For most of human history, this type of art – naturalism – has been the exception rather than the rule. And in fact Renaissance naturalism only gradually replaced various medieval styles which reflected a very different outlook – for example, the use of solemn, stylized images against a gold background, designed to intensify religious devotion. The naturalistic tradition, established during the Renaissance, remained the norm in western art right down to the 20th century.

The visual arts were only one aspect of the Italian Renaissance, which was a new way of life, affecting everything from scholarship and statecraft to etiquette and fashion. Put crudely, where the Middle Ages had been otherworldly or heaven-centred, the Renaissance was this-worldly or human-centred. There was a new confidence in human potential, and 'Man can do all things' became received doctrine. Individual excellence was intensely admired and fame was ardently pursued.

Much of this can be sensed in Renaissance paintings and sculptures. For example, the 15th century was the first great age of portraiture since ancient times seeking to capture the distinctive traits of an individual rather than to present a generalized image of power or piety. On the other hand, as the illustrations in this book demonstrate, the Renaissance was not worldly in the sense of being indifferent to religion; but religion itself had become warmer, more human and more aware of the beauty of God's creation. Artists responded by showing biblical episodes in a new way, as dramas of human love and suffering.

A striking feature of the Renaissance was that people realized that they were living in an age of great achievement, but thought of it in terms of a revival rather than as something new. Although they never actually used the word Renaissance (French for 'rebirth'), this describes their outlook very accurately. Ungratefully despising the immediate past, they saw themselves as returning to the values of Classical Antiquity – the civilization of ancient Greece and Rome.

The impact of classicism on the visual arts can be seen in the Roman-style, round-arched buildings that feature in paintings and reliefs, in the popularity of mythological scenes, and above all in the reappearance of the nude in western art. The naked body, in the Middle Ages almost always an object of shame, became the most expressive of all forms in the works of an artist such as Michelangelo. The emphasis on physical splendour – beautiful, perfectly proportioned men and women – also derives from the classical tradition as the Renaissance understood it.

New aims called for the development of new skills. Around 1400, artists began to master the science of perspective, which helped them to create convincing three-dimensional appearances on flat surfaces; other aids to naturalism were modelling by using light and shade, and the study of anatomy. There were also exciting technical advances in bronze casting, wall painting (the fresco technique, using fresh, still-damp plaster) and panel painting, where oils (an import from Flanders) gradually supplanted the older tempera medium; and towards the end of the Renaissance the easel painting – done in oil paints on canvas – was introduced.

The achievements of the Renaissance are bound up with the development of thriving cities such as Florence, Rome and Venice – independent centres with wealthy citizens and civic and religious authorities, eager to beautify them and outdo their rivals. Florence produced more great artists than any other centre, but the climax of the Renaissance – the 'High Renaissance' – took place in early 16th-century Rome, where papal munificence created unparalleled opportunities for work on the grand scale by Michelangelo, Raphael and others. The Renaissance impulse flagged from about 1530, although Venetian art retained its full vigour until late in the century. But long before then the Renaissance had crossed the Alps and was conquering Europe.

▷ The Annunciation 1333
Simone Martini (1284-1344)

Panel

THE CITY OF SIENA was the rival of Florence, in art among other things, developing its own strong traditions. Simone Martini was a great Sienese master who worked in the courtly International Gothic style, so called because it was practised in a number of European countries. By contrast with the naturalism of Giotto, Simone's art is refined and ceremonious, with charming, elongated figures and a wealth of poetic details; it too contributed to the development of the Renaissance style. *The Annunciation* is part of an altarpiece painted for a chapel in Siena Cathedral. It pictures the moment when the Archangel Gabriel tells the Virgin Mary of her special destiny, and her first impulse is to shrink away. Simone had a spectacularly successful career, working in his native Siena and at Assisi, and becoming painter to the king of Naples before being summoned to the papal court at Avignon, where he spent his last years.

△ The Lamentation c.1310
Giotto di Bondone (c.1266-1337)

Fresco

GIOTTO WAS THE GREAT forerunner of the Italian Renaissance. His contemporaries had no doubt that he had revived the art of painting, and he was so famous that he worked all over Italy as well as in his native Florence. The most celebrated of all his surviving works is the cycle of frescoes in the Scrovegni (or Arena) Chapel at Padua. *The Lamentation* shows the radical nature of Giotto's break with the stylized, static, other-worldly Byzantine painting that had previously dominated Italian art. Despite the presence of angels and gold haloes, this is a poignant human drama, with solid figures set in real space. Jesus has just been taken down from the cross. His mother cradles his head in her lap while Mary Magdalene holds his pierced feet. All the actors are absorbed in their reactions to the dead Christ; two of them even have their backs to us.

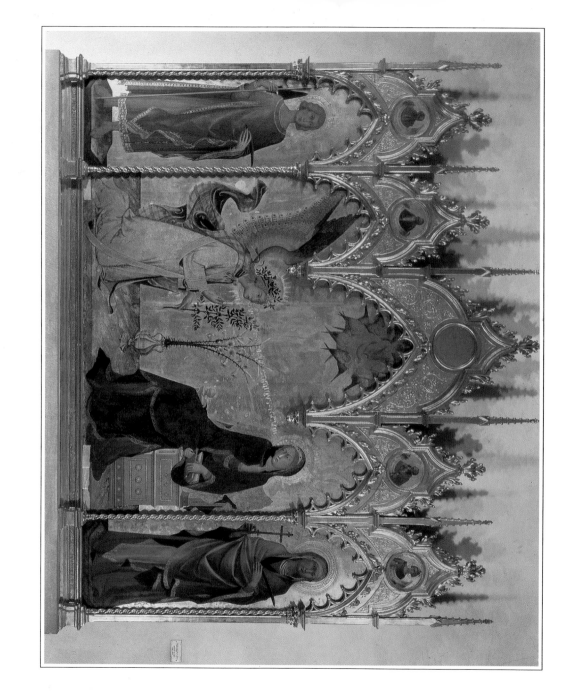

△ **The Story of Jacob and Esau**
Cast in 1452
Lorenzo Ghiberti (1378-1455)

Bronze

DESPITE THE PIONEERING
genius of Giotto, the history of
Renaissance art really begins
in early 15th century Florence.
It might well be dated to 1401,
the year in which an open
competition was held to decide
who would be commissioned
to make a set of grand bronze
doors for the cathedral
baptistery. The winning trial
piece was submitted by
Ghiberti, who then spent the
years 1403-24 on this task. The
completed doors, whose
panels are filled with scenes
from the New Testament, were
greeted with acclaim, and
Ghiberti was immediately
contracted for a second set of
doors with Old Testament
scenes. Made between 1425
and 1452, these were later
nicknamed 'the Gates of
Paradise' by Michelangelo. *The
Story of Jacob and Esau* shows
how thoroughly Ghiberti
mastered the new art of
perspective. The influence of
classical art appears in both
the modelling of the figures
and the architectural style.

△ **The Tribute Money** c.1425
Masaccio (1401-1429?)

Fresco

DURING THE 14TH CENTURY
Giotto's influence in Florence
faded, and the decorative
Gothic style of painting
enjoyed a long vogue.
Renaissance naturalism was
reinvented in the 1420s,
almost single-handedly by a
man nicknamed Masaccio.
With its monumental, light-
modelled forms and calculated
perspective effects, *The Tribute
Money* is probably his best
known work, one of a group in
the Florentine church of Santa
Maria del Carmine. As in
Giotto's paintings (page 8), the
Gospel narrative is rendered
in human and dramatic terms,
though the austere style is
Masaccio's own. The subject is
a miracle performed by Jesus
at Capernaum, where he told
his disciple Peter that he
would find the money for a
local tax in the mouth of a fish.
The central scene shows the
confrontation with the tax
collector; on the left Peter
finds the money and on the
right pays the tax. Masaccio
left Florence for Rome in
1428, and was never heard
of again.

▽ **David** c.1430
Donatello (1386-1466)

Bronze

LIKE SO MANY Renaissance artists, the Florentine sculptor Donato di Niccolo Bardi became known by a nickname, in his case Donatello. He learned his craft from Ghiberti (page 10), developing into a master who combined a feeling for physical splendour with emotional intensity. *David* was a revolutionary work both technically and culturally. The first large, free-standing nude since antiquity, it implicitly contradicted the medieval conviction that nakedness was a cause for shame; and although the subject is the biblical slayer of Goliath (whose head lies at David's feet), Donatello makes him more like a Greek god than a Hebrew shepherd. Although bronze-casting techniques were highly developed for making cannon, they were not applied to ambitious works of art until this time. The *David* and Donatello's great equestrian statue at Padua showed that the Renaissance artist could equal, and surpass, the admired works of antiquity.

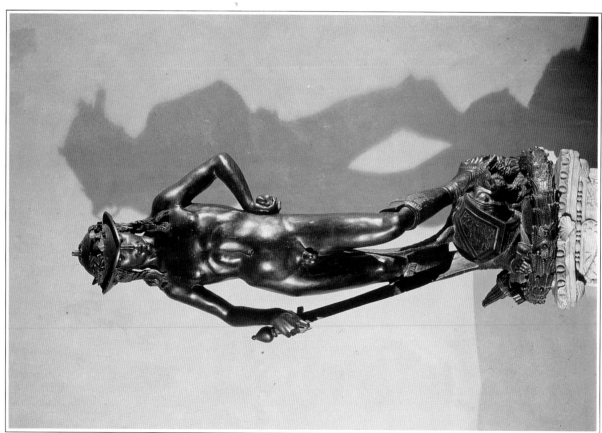

△ **The Battle of San Romano** 1430s Paolo Uccello (1397-1475)

Panel

DESPITE HIS LONG LIFE, only a few works by Uccello are known. This may reflect a erratic career, for there is evidence that Uccello was an eccentric character, capable of letting his clients down. He is said to have spent an inordinate amount of time studying the new Renaissance science of perspective, which enabled artists to produce convincingly natural-looking scenes. In *The Battle of San Romano*, Uccello consciously shows off his perspective skills, for example in aligning the broken lance shafts on the ground to suggest parallels that will meet at the horizon. However, he also uses perspective for his own idiosyncratic purposes, as part of a patterned, decorative approach to painting. This is one of three panels picturing different phases of a battle between the forces of Florence and Siena, fought in 1432; it shows the climax, when the Sienese commander has been unhorsed and his men are turning tail. In the busy background, no doubt to mock the defeated enemy, greyhounds are pursuing terrified hares.

▽ **The Transfiguration** c.1440
Fra Angelico (c.1400-1455)

Fresco

FRA GIOVANNI DA FIESOLE was a Dominican friar who became the head of his convent and was widely admired as a person and as an artist; his services as a painter were much in demand, and he made several working trips to Rome, dying there on the last of them. The most extraordinary of Fra Angelico's works are in the monastery of San Marco in Florence, now a museum with a unique atmosphere: he and his assistants decorated the entire building with paintings, including one in each cell, intended for private contemplation. Though there are pre-Renaissance elements in Angelico's delightful, often ethereal figures, he absorbed Florentine innovations such as perspective, and evidently learned from his younger (and shorter-lived) contemporary, Masaccio (page 13). *The Transfiguration* shows him in sterner mood, picturing a large, majestic Jesus appearing to the apostles in a blaze of light.

Madonna and Child with Angels c.1455   Fra Filippo Lippi (c.1406-1469)

Panel

◁ Previous page 17

THE IRONIC CONTRAST between art and life is particularly marked in the case of Fra Filippo, poetic painter and sinful monk. He may well have taken vows to escape grinding poverty. In the 1420s he became a painter, deeply influenced by Masaccio. By the 1450s he was in deep trouble, having fathered a child on a nun, Lucrezia Buti, and he faced trial and torture on account of his financial misdemeanours. Filippo was eventually rescued through the influence of Cosimo de'Medici, renounced his vows, married Lucrezia, and continued to paint religious subjects. At first heavily indebted to Masaccio's powerful forms and dramatic use of light and shadow (page 13), Filippo evolved a very different style of his own, sweet, airy and brightly coloured, which he passed on to his pupil, Botticelli. Whether this is religious art is another matter. For all her charming gravity, Filippo's Virgin is a beauty dressed in the height of mid-century Florentine fashion; while the wings of the cheeky urchin-angel look appropriately insecure.

△ The Virgin and Child with Saints c.1445   Domenico Veneziano (c.1410-1461)

Panel

AS HIS NAME INDICATES, Domenico Veneziano was a native of Venice, a great commercial and maritime city which was not yet a major art centre. Little is known of Domenico's life until 1439, when he arrived to work in Florence. He absorbed Florentine technical discoveries, but retained an unFlorentine taste for exquisite colour and light effects. *The Virgin and Child with Saints*, also known as the *St Lucy altarpiece*, is an early example of the *sacra conversazione* ('holy conversation'), grouping rather than isolating the figures on altarpieces. This development reflected the greater intimacy and human warmth of religious attitudes. Appropriately, one of the figures in Domenico's painting is St Francis of Assisi, whose example had done so much to humanize religion. The other saints are John the Baptist, Zenobius and St Lucy, holding out the platter on which, traditionally, she presented the eyes she had plucked out and sent to a profane admirer; fortunately the Virgin rewarded her by restoring them.

△ **The Flagellation of Christ** c.1445
Piero della Francesca (c.1410-1492)

Panel

PIERO WAS BORN and died in the little town of Borgo San Sepulcro. In a period when artists were trying to capture action and emotion, he created an art of formal beauty and monumental, mysterious stillness. *The Flagellation* shows Jesus being flogged as a prelude to his crucifixion. Strangely, the flogging takes place towards the back of the picture space, while the main subject appears to be the conversation between three men in the foreground to the right, one of them bare-footed. Piero's use of perspective is so accurate that the entire scene can be reconstructed in three dimensions with models; but none of the many explanations of its meaning and purpose has yet been generally accepted.

▷ **Portrait of Federico da Montefeltro** (Detail) c.1475
Piero della Francesca

Panel

THE INDEPENDENT city-state of Urbino was close to Piero's native town, and this splendid portrait is one of a number of works he painted for its ruler, Federico da Montefeltro – possibly including the celebrated *Flagellation* (page 20). Small though it was, Urbino became one of the great centres of Renaissance culture, thanks to Federico and his successors. The 'portrait' is actually a detail from an altarpiece showing the Virgin and saints; as its donor, Federico is represented in the scene, a humble but also a very prominent presence. His hands and helmet, painted in a rather different style from the rest of the picture, are believed to be the work of another artist, Pedro Berruguete. The armour is appropriate, since Federico financed his court by fighting for wealthier princes. The profile view of him served to conceal the fact that a sword blow had cost him his right eye, though its impact on the bridge of his nose could not be concealed.

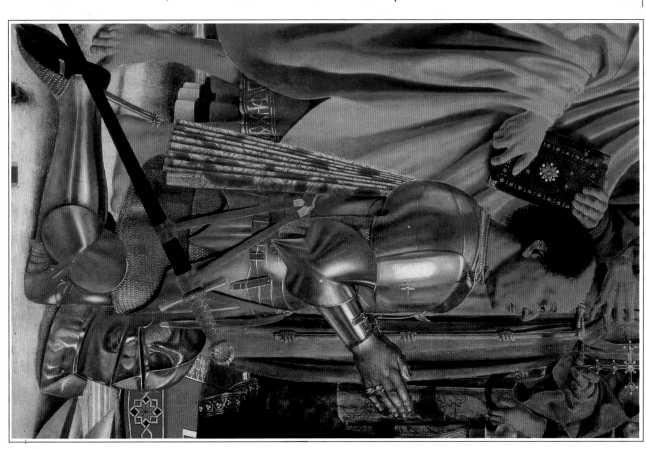

△ The Journey of the Magi
c.1459
Benozzo Gozzoli (1420–97)

Fresco

THE NOMINAL SUBJECT of this fresco is the journey made by the wise men from the East, following a star, to pay homage to the new-born Jesus. Long before Benozzo's day, tradition had turned the wise men, or Magi, into kings whom artists could show in all their finery, contrasted with the humble circumstances of the Holy Family. Benozzo, by picturing the journey rather than its culmination, makes the scene one of purely worldly ostentation. In fact this is really a procession of Renaissance magnificos, featuring members of Florence's ruling Medici family and their followers. The landscape resembles the countryside around Florence, and Benozzo's treatment might stand as an advertisement for the new Renaissance skills of perspective and figure painting. Benozzo started as an assistant to the great religious painter Fra Angelico, but the essentially secular *Journey of the Magi* was the high point of his career.

St Jerome in his Study c.1460
Antonello da Messina
(c.1430-1479)

Panel

▷ *Overleaf page 24*

DISCOVERIES SUCH AS the rules of perspective enabled the Renaissance artist to create the illusion that his painted surface belonged to the world of three-dimensional reality. Taken to its limit, illusionism could deceive the eye (*trompe l'œil*), for example by framing the picture in architecture that seemed real, directing the spectator's gaze through it into what appeared to be an extension of real space. Here, the fictive architectural framework is all the more convincing because birds strut on the 'outermost' ledge; beyond, we can see St Jerome in a grand vaulted room, and through the far windows a landscape stretches away into the distance. Antonello was one of the earliest Italian artists to absorb the influence of Flemish art, in which meticulously accurate detail and illusionistic effects were made possible by the development of painting in oils.

▽ The Doge Leonardo Loredano c.1501
Giovanni Bellini (c.1426-1516)

Panel

LEONARDO LOREDANO became Doge of Venice in 1501, at the age of seventy-five, and held office until his death in 1521. Venice was an oligarchy, with the Doge as the nominal head of state; but the title had great prestige, crowning a man's career. Loredano's costume is lovingly painted, but its silken texture and elaborate pattern are dominated by his severe, lined face. Though Bellini has broken with the profile convention which dominated early Renaissance portraiture, the portrait of the Doge, the painting is cut off across the chest so that it resembles a carved portrait bust. As usual, Venice lagged behind Florentine fashion, which already permitted half-length portraits showing the hands. The almost contemporary *Mona Lisa* showed how relaxed and informal the result could be – but that would hardly have done for this masterpiece of Bellini's old age, in which the Doge's tightly closed garment accentuates his authority and steely self-discipline.

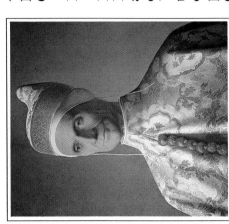

▽ *Previous page 25*

The Agony in the Garden 1460s
Giovanni Bellini (c.1426-1516)

Panel

THREE OF THE OUTSTANDING Venetian painters of the 15th century came from the same family. The work of Jacopo Bellini (c.1400-c.1470) was of such a high quality that his more famous sons, Gentile (c.1429-1507) and Giovanni, used his drawings and compositional schemes even in their maturity. Gentile was a great traveller, while Giovanni stayed at home, running a large workshop and eventually becoming the official state painter. Both Gentile and Giovanni were strongly influenced by their young brother-in-law, Mantegna (page 28). In the mid-1450s he painted *Agony in the Garden*, showing Jesus praying in the garden of Gethsemane on the night before his crucifixion. The picture, in Mantegna's most sculpturesque manner, evidently provoked Giovanni to produce an equivalent in his softer, more atmospheric style, bathing the scene in early morning light and including many charming landscape details. Nevertheless this is a sombre moment, for the soldiers are already on their way, led by Judas, to arrest Jesus.

△ **The Meeting** c.1473
Andrea Mantegna
(c.1431-1506)

Fresco

IN 1460 MANTEGNA settled at Mantua, where he became court painter to the Marchese Ludovico Gonzago. Like Urbino (page 21), Mantua was a small principality whose highly cultivated rulers made a disproportionately large contribution to the Renaissance. For the rest of his long life Mantegna worked for the Gonzagas. The most spectacular of all his works is the *Camera degli Sposi* (or *Camera Picta*) in the Castello at Mantua. His frescoes comprise a family cycle, celebrating the doings of the Gonzagas, including the meeting between Marchese Ludovico and his son Cardinal Francesco. The individual scenes are most impressive seen in the chamber, for they are part of a total experience in which the painted space seems to extend to the horizon and, in the dome, the ceiling is painted so that it seems to be open to the sky and to be topped by a balcony from which people look down on the spectators below.

The Dead Christ
Andrea Mantegna (c.1431-1506)

Canvas

▽ *Previous page 27*

MANTEGNA WAS THE MOST important North Italian painter of the 15th century. He was born near Padua, where he is first heard of, working on a series of frescoes for a church, in the late 1440s. He developed a new painting style in which the forms were as solid, distinct and hard-edged as sculpture; and in fact Donatello (page 14), who worked in Padua, was probably the major influence on Mantegna. His 'stoney manner' is very much in evidence in the figure of the dead Christ resting on a marble slab. It is a celebrated example of foreshortening – perspective technique applied to a single object so that it appears to recede into the imaginary space of the picture. This is not simply a piece of Renaissance virtuosity, since the converse is that the figure seems to be thrusting out at the spectator, demanding an adequate response. Experts differ violently over the dating of the picture. Mantegna never parted with it, so it may have been painted for his private devotions.

▽ The Martyrdom of St Sebastian c.1475
Antonio Pollaiuolo
(c.1432-1498)

Panel

ANTONIO AND HIS BROTHER
Piero (c.1441-1496) ran one of the leading workshops in Florence. Antonio seems to have been far more talented, and probably painted almost all of this great altarpiece; Piero may have been responsible for the rather characterless face of the saint. Sebastian is said to have been a Roman officer who served in the guard of the persecuting emperor Diocletian; when he refused to renounce his Christian beliefs, he was shot to death with arrows.

Pollaiuolo takes advantage of the subject to display his anatomical expertise, drawing our attention away from the saint to the archers, straining to wind up their crossbows or firing at point-blank range into the body of the unlucky Sebastian. The Roman ruin, and the Florentine landscape stretching into the far distance, are painted with considerable panache.

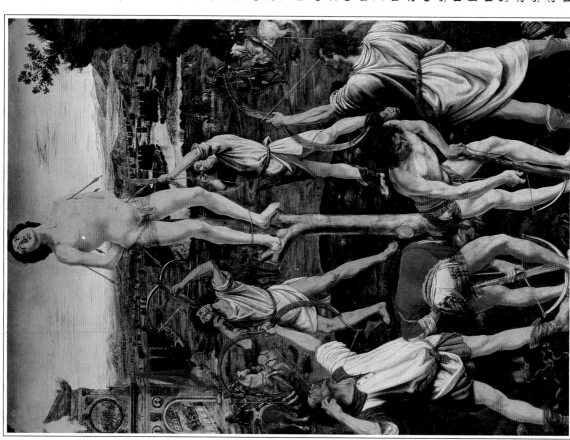

▷ **The Baptism of Christ**
c.1470
Andrea del Verrocchio
(1435-88)

Panel

VERROCCHIO, AN ARTIST of
stature, was also influential as
the master of a Florentine
workshop which numbered
among its assistants Lorenzo di
Credi and Leonardo da Vinci.
Verrocchio himself was
primarily a sculptor, his career
culminating in a commission
for a great equestrian statue in
Venice, the Colleoni
Monument. His best-known
painting shows Jesus being
baptized by his forerunner,
John the Baptist. Both men
are ankle-deep in water, and
while John performs the
ceremony a dove representing
the Holy Spirit hovers
overhead. However, most
interest in the picture has
centred on the two boy-angels,
because the left-hand figure is
generally held to have been
painted by Leonardo da Vinci.
By contrast with Verrocchio's
boy-in-the-street, Leonardo's
has a typically soulful
expression, flowing hair and
voluminous, beautifully
draped robes. The landscape
above the angels' heads is also

attributed to Leonardo. On
seeing his apprentice's work
Verrocchio is said to have
given up painting in despair –
an appropriate, if unlikely,
response.

△ **The Adoration of the Magi** c.1476
Sandro Botticelli (1445-1510)

Panel

BOTTICELLI, one of the leading
Florentine painters of the late
15th century, was forgotten or
ignored until the 19th century;
yet since then, his delicate line,
vivid colours and command of
poetic atmosphere have made
him a popular favourite.
Though best known for
mythological paintings such as
The Birth of Venus (page 34), he
produced many religious
works, including several
Adorations. The Magi were the
wise men who followed a star to
find the new-born Jesus. This is
Botticelli's most ambiguous
treatment of the subject, for the
Magi can be identified as
members of the Medici family
which dominated the
Florentine state; in fact the
scene might almost be a
continuation of Benozzo
Gozzoli's *Journey of the Magi*
(page 22), with many of the
entourage continuing to show
off despite the nature of the
occasion. The Virgin and Child,
however, are portrayed with a
sweet seriousness characteristic
of Botticelli. The man on the
right, gazing out at us, is
believed to be a self-portrait.

△ **The Birth of Venus** c.1482
Sandro Botticelli (1445–1510)

Canvas

THIS CELEBRATED PICTURE is
based on the legend that
Venus, the goddess of love, was
born from the foam of the sea.
Here she is carried to the shore
on a shell, blown forward by
figures representing the winds;
an attendant waits to drape a
cloak over her. *The Birth of
Venus* was the first Renaissance
painting based squarely on
classical mythology but its
atmosphere hardly seems
pagan or sensual, and was
never intended to be so. Like
Botticelli's almost equally
famous *Primavera* (Spring), it
was commissioned by the
Medici, who combined political
with intellectual and artistic
interests. They favoured a
philosophy, Neoplatonism, that
was designed to reconcile
classical and Christian ideas,
interpreting the gods of
ancient Greece and Rome as
mystical or symbolic beings. So
Botticelli's Venus probably
symbolizes love or beauty in its
widest, most spiritual sense;
and many other elements in
the painting probably have
arcane symbolic meanings.

△ **Christ giving the Keys to St Peter** 1481
Perugino (c.1448-1523)

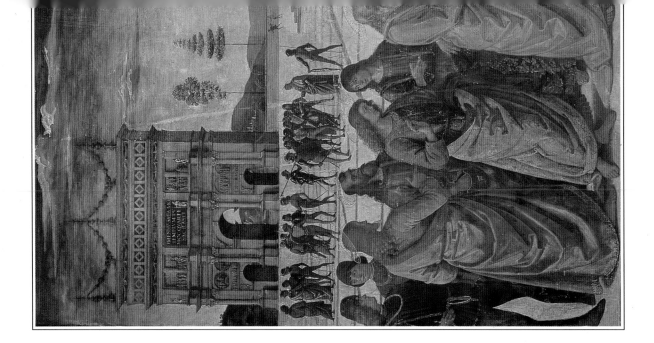

Fresco

PERUGINO (Pietro Vanucci) was nicknamed after his home town, Perugia. By the early 1470s he was working in Florence, but in 1479 he moved to Rome, where he was employed painting frescoes for the newly built Sistine Chapel. The chapel is now best known for the ceiling and altar wall painted by Michelangelo on the orders of Pope Julius II; but earlier artists (Perugino, Ghirlandaio, Botticelli) also made distinguished contributions to its decoration. The fresco shown here is typical of Perugino's stately, clear, straightforward compositions and undramatic style. Christ hands St Peter the keys which symbolize his supreme authority over the Church; the implication is that Peter's successors as bishops of Rome – the popes – have inherited his role. Perugino prospered for a time and Raphael (pages 56-61) was his pupil (c.1500-c.1504). But his style went out of fashion and from 1506 he worked in relative obscurity in Perugia.

▽ **An Old Man and a Boy**
c.1480
Domenico Ghirlandaio
(1449-94)

Panel

IN HIS DAY Ghirlandaio was a highly successful artist with a big Florentine workshop and more commissions than he and his assistants could comfortably handle; the great Michelangelo was one of his apprentices. Ghirlandaio's reputation has fluctuated over the centuries, and at times, despite his sound workmanship and fine colour sense, he has been dismissed as prosaic. However, his very popular *Old Man and a Boy* shows how much poetry can be found in the ordinary. The tender feeling between the two figures has given rise to the idea that they are grandfather and grandson, although this remains unprovable. Thanks to Ghirlandaio's sobriety of treatment, the old man's deformed nose seems no more than a true detail, rather than one intended to give the picture an idiosyncratic quality. The simplicity of the interior is nicely balanced by the mysterious and fascinating landscape.

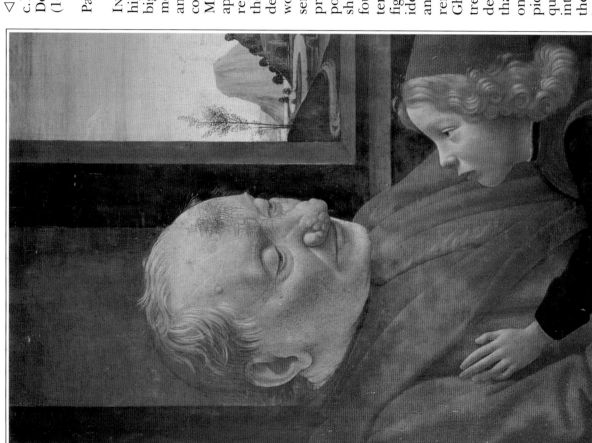

▷ The Departure of Aeneas Silvius Piccolomini for Basel
1503-8
Pintoricchio (c.1454-1513)

Fresco

PINTORICCHIO came from Perugia, and c.1480 worked with Perugino (page 36) on the frescoes in the Sistine Chapel. Though influenced by Perugino, his mature work was in a more cheerfully decorative style. Pintoricchio's largest commission was a cycle of frescoes in the Piccolomini Library in Siena Cathedral, celebrating the life of the library's founder, Aeneas Silvius Piccolomini (1405-64) combined a devotion to classical studies with a career in the Church, ultimately becoming Pius II. *The Departure of Piccolomini* appears to be taking place just outside the room, since it is viewed through a superbly elaborate arch, which is actually part of the painted surface. The future pope is about to set out from Genoa for the Church council at Basel. The liveliness of the scene makes up for a certain blandness in the faces; the company appear to be more conscious of the spectator than of the storm that is blowing up.

△ **The Dream of St Ursula** 1495
Vittore Carpaccio (c.1460-1526)

Canvas

ALMOST NOTHING is known about Carpaccio's life until the 1490s, when he painted a cycle of large pictures showing episodes from the life of St Ursula; it was done for the charitable foundation named after her, the Scuola di Sant'Orsola in Venice. The story follows Ursula's betrothal to a British prince who converted to Christianity in order to win her; her pilgrimage to Rome as the leader of 11,011 virgins; and the murder of the entire party by the Huns. In *The Dream of St Ursula* her impending martyrdom is announced by the arrival of an angel. But the charm of the painting – and of Carpaccio as a narrative painter – lies in the meticulous details: Ursula herself neatly tucked-up, her slippers, her little dog, and the crown discarded at the foot of the bed, presumably ready to be put on first thing in the morning. Carpaccio worked for a number of *scuole*, but from the early 1500s he was overshadowed by Titian and his career petered out.

A Mythological Scene c.1510
Piero di Cosimo (1462-1521)

Panel

▷ *Overleaf page 42*

PIERO DI COSIMO was an eccentric, and his contemporaries enjoyed telling stories about him – that, for instance, he lived on eggs, which he hard-boiled in batches of 50. He also allowed his garden to run wild, a very odd trait at a time when the essence of a garden was held to be its artificiality, representing the conquest of nature. Though Piero was famous for inventive public works such as tableaux, his paintings are intensely poetic and mysterious. This one has sometimes been labelled *The Death of Procris*, relating it to the Greek myth in which Procris was accidentally killed by her hunter husband, who mistook her for his quarry. However, the identification does not fit in too well with the scene painted by Piero, in which the chief mourners are a Pan-like being and a dog, neither of whom fully understands what has happened. In any event, the 'programme' seems less important than the gently sorrowful atmosphere, pointed up by the lovely background and its inhabitants.

△ **Lady with an Ermine** c.1483
Leonardo da Vinci (1452-1519)

Panel

LEONARDO, the illegitimate son of a notary, was born in the little Tuscan town of Vinci. He was apprenticed to Verrocchio in Florence, where his prodigious gifts were quickly revealed (page 31).

Passionately interested in art, science and technology, he moved rapidly from one project to the next, astounding his contemporaries. By 1483 he had settled in Milan, working for its ruler, Lodovico Sforza, as musician, military engineer, painter, sculptor and cultural master of ceremonies. Not long after his arrival, Leonardo painted this portrait, whose subject is almost certainly Lodovico's teenage mistress, Cecilia Gallerani. Repainting by some later artist has given Leonardo's work a hard-edged look, but it is still a tender but unpatronizing study of extreme youth encased in Renaissance formality. Cecilia's pose, with her head and body at slightly different angles, represents an advance in sophistication on earlier types of portraiture.

△ **The Last Supper** 1498   Leonardo da Vinci (1452-1519)

Wall painting

LIKE THE RUINS of antiquity, Leonardo's *Last Supper* has an enduring fascination. When it was painted, he was already famous, having modelled a 'Great Horse' of clay, ready for casting in bronze. *The Last Supper* was another triumph, treating with a new dramatic intensity the moment when Jesus announced that one of his disciples, present in the room, would betray him. Protesting,

arguing among themselves, shrinking backwards in dismay or half-rising, the disciples interact with one another in a way that had never been seen before. Tragically, neither of Leonardo's masterworks remained intact. The Great Horse was never cast, and was eventually destroyed by French soldiers. *The Last Supper* began to deteriorate almost as soon as it was finished, because

Leonardo had tried to improve on the received wallpainting technique (fresco), substituting an oil mixture and clay support for water-based paints and plaster. Over the centuries, repaintings and attempted restorations did nothing to help matters; they have been stripped away, and we can now at least glimpse the greatness of Leonardo's most ambitious work.

△ **Mona Lisa** c.1503
Leonardo da Vinci
(1452-1519)

Canvas

THE *Mona Lisa* is so famous that it is hard to see it with fresh eyes. One thing is certain: the mysterious charm of the woman's smile is not a modern fancy. The Renaissance biographer Giorgio Vasari, writing only a few years after Leonardo's death, described it as 'divine rather than human', and claimed that the artist kept her in an agreeable humour by employing musicians and jesters to perform while he painted. Despite dirt and varnish, the portrait is still wonderfully alive and convincing. The characteristic Leonardo background of mist and rocks gives it a romantic quality, enhanced by the way in which figure and landscape are integrated. 'Mona' is simply a contraction of the respectful form of address 'Madonna' (Lady), in this case the wife of a wealthy merchant who commissioned the painting. Leonardo worked on it for four years, decided not to part with it, and took it with him to France in 1516.

▷ **The Virgin of the Rocks**
1508
Leonardo da Vinci
(1452-1519)

Panel

IN APRIL 1483 LEONARDO contracted to supply an altarpiece for a chapel in Milan. He painted a version of the stipulated subject which is now in the Louvre Museum in Paris. It was never delivered to the church, no doubt because Leonardo became involved in a dispute over the terms of the contract. It was finally settled in 1506, and in 1508 he delivered the painting. However, it was not the Louvre version but a new work (National Gallery, London). The compositions are basically similar, but in style and atmosphere they belong to separate epochs – an almost unique situation, given the fact that they were painted by the same man. Whereas the Louvre version is warmer and softer, the National Gallery painting announces the High Renaissance – the quarter of a century in which Italian Renaissance art culminated in works of supreme technical skill and a mood of solemnity and classical grandeur.

△ **Pietà** 1500
Michelangelo Buonarroti
(1475-1564)

Marble

AT 13 MICHELANGELO was apprenticed to Ghirlandaio in Florence, and he was still in his teens when he was taken into the household of the city's rulers, the Medici, to study and create. But his first undisputed masterpieces were produced after the deteriorating political situation in Florence had persuaded him to move to Rome. A French cardinal, Jean Villiers, commissioned Michelangelo to carve a *pietà* for the chapel of the French kings in St Peter's. A *pietà* is a representation of the Virgin Mary cradling the crucified Christ in her lap; at the time, the subject was a relative novelty in Italian art, and especially hard for a sculptor to bring off with any degree of realism. Michelangelo's *Pietà* is at once visually convincing, emotionally powerful and, in the treatment of the drapery, a work of conscious virtuosity. The youthfulness of the Virgin is a curious, much-discussed feature of the *Pietà*.

David 1504
Michelangelo Buonarroti (1475-1564)

Marble

◁ Previous page 49

IN 1501 MICHELANGELO left Rome for Florence, where a new republican system seemed to have ended the conflicts of the previous decades. He may have hurried back on hearing of proposals to use 'the Giant', a huge block of marble which had been standing in the city for more than a generation. Michelangelo was commissioned to carve from it a colossal statue of David, the biblical hero who slew the Philistine champion Goliath;

David was a symbol of Florence, and the commission was a political act, expressing a renewed republican self-confidence. Michelangelo's *David* was received with rapture, as a work that equalled, or even surpassed, the physical splendour of classical sculpture. At the same time, *David* is post-classical in its psychological tension and sense of imminent violence, as the young man stands ready for action with his sling over his shoulder.

△ **The Holy Family** 1504
Michelangelo Buonarroti
(1475-1564)

Panel

ALSO KNOWN as the *Doni Tondo*. A tondo is a circular painting or relief; the shape was fashionable in the 15th century for devotional works hung in private houses. Around 1504 Michelangelo carved two *tondi* as well as painting *The Holy Family*. Although he had already produced masterpieces of sculpture, including the *Pietà* and *David* (pages 48-9), this is the earliest known painting by him. It is reminiscent of sculpture in the solidity of the figures, firm-fleshed under a metallic light, and in the close-knit grouping of Mary, Joseph and the infant Jesus. A horizontal band separates the family from the young John the Baptist, perhaps indicating the dividing line between the new dispensation, ushered in by Christ, and the old order. However, the figures behind John are not Hebrew prophets but nudes in the classical tradition – perhaps included for no more cogent reason than Michelangelo's passion for the human body as a vehicle for artistic expression.

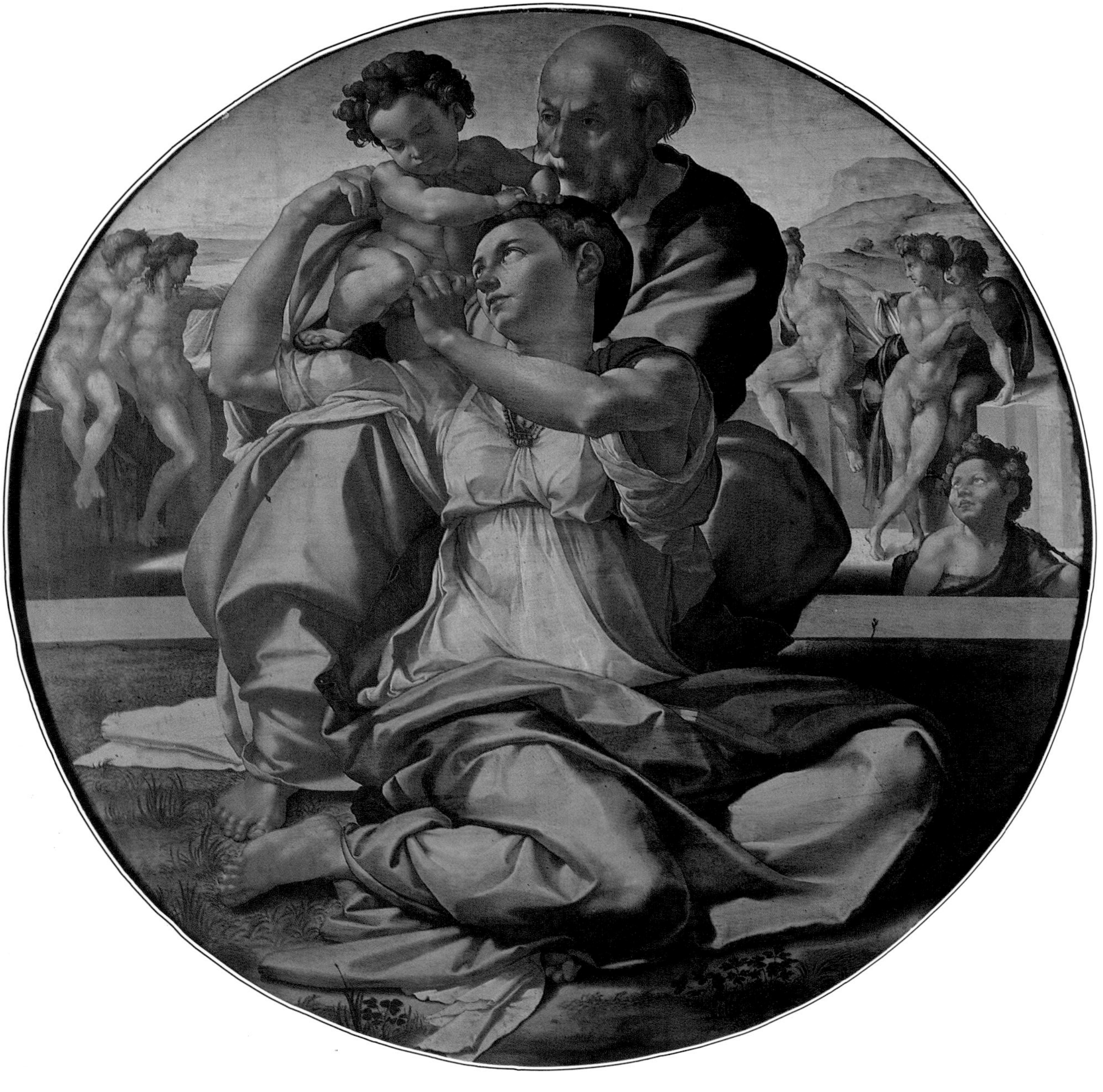

△ **The Creation of Adam**
1511
Michelangelo Buonarroti
(1475-1564)

Fresco

IN 1504 MICHELANGELO was summoned to Rome, where he began a turbulent nine-year association with Pope Julius II. In 1508 Julius asked him to paint a series of apostles on the ceiling of the Sistine Chapel. According to his own account, Michelangelo protested that he was a sculptor, not a painter; but once persuaded to accept, he extended his original commission until he had covered the entire ceiling (some 520 square metres) with a series of biblical scenes, framed by painted architecture and surrounded by powerful nude figures, sybils and prophets. In October 1512, after almost four years of toil, this vast, heroic work was shown to the world, which hailed 'the divine Michelangelo' as the master of masters. *The Creation of Adam* is one of the culminating scenes at the altar end of the chapel. God's touch pours life into a still-languid Adam; Eve, already potentially in existence, lies beneath the Creator's arm.

△ **Sinners Cast Down into Hell** 1541
Michelangelo Buonarroti (1475-1564)

Fresco

THIS IS A DETAIL from *The Last Judgement*, a fresco which Michelangelo painted on the entire altar wall of the Sistine Chapel on the orders of Pope Paul III. In mood it is very different from the great ceiling (page 52-3), reflecting the changes that had taken place in Michelangelo's life and in the wider history of Italy. As he grew older, Michelangelo became more preoccupied with sin and salvation, his mood matching that of Italian society as the Counter-Reformation gained strength.

Though Christ is shown separating the saved from the damned, the overwhelming impression is one of terror rather than joy; the pope himself, when he saw the fresco, fell on his knees and cried out in fear. The human body is no longer shown as beautiful and splendid, but the nudity of the figures still offended Counter-Reformation puritanism, and in the 1550s their modesty was restored with wisps of drapery.

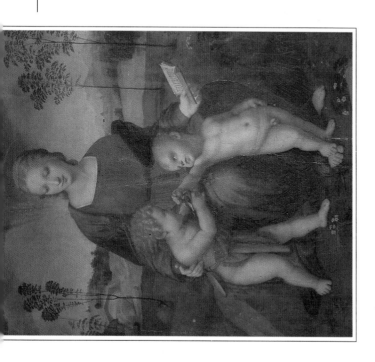

△ The Madonna of the Goldfinch 1506
Raphael (1483-1520)

Panel

RAFFAELLO SANZIO was the youthful prodigy of the High Renaissance, achieving a status equal to that of Leonardo and Michelangelo while still in his twenties, only to die at the age of 37. He was born at Urbino, the son of a painter, and worked for Perugino, whose ample, orderly compositions (page 36) certainly influenced him. Between about 1504 and 1508 Raphael appears to have spent most of his time in Florence, absorbing Leonardo's innovations and painting a long series of Madonnas. Raphael's reputation has fluctuated rather more than those of Leonardo and Michelangelo, although it now seems to have become firmly re-established. The large figures, pyramidal composition and majestic calm of *The Madonna of the Goldfinch* mark it as a pioneering work of the High Renaissance.

△ **Portrait of Baldassare Castiglione** c.1515
Raphael (1483-1520)

Canvas

RAPHAEL WAS ARGUABLY the first modern portraitist, technically equipped to produce a convincing likeness and (at least as important) prepared to subordinate his personality to that of the sitter. The calm assurance of Castiglione (1478-1529) is entirely in character, since he was a diplomat who died at the height of his career, representing the pope at the Spanish court. He was even more celebrated as the author of *The Book of the Courtier*, the first manual aiming to teach its readers how to become accomplished men of the world; the production of such self-help literature was one of the hallmarks of the Renaissance. Castiglione's ideal gentleman was characterized in all his did by *sprezzatura*, ability displayed with an apparent lack of effort – 'the art that conceals art'. Castiglione's friend Raphael had just such a gift for making even his greatest achievements look simple and straightforward.

The School of Athens 1511
Raphael (1483-1520)

Fresco

◁ *Previous page*

LATE IN 1508 RAPHAEL went to Rome, and within months was employed to decorate the new apartments being prepared for Pope Julius II in the Vatican. In the very first room, the Stanza della Segnatura, Raphael painted a set of frescos representing the four great branches of Renaissance learning – literature, philosophy, jurisprudence and theology. He brought these abstract subjects to life by creating pseudo-historical scenes filled with imaginary portraits of Renaissance culture-heroes. In *Philosophy*, better known as *The School of Athens*, Plato and Aristotle appear at the top of a set of steps, surrounded by the famous thinkers of antiquity, who are deep in thought or engaged in animated discussion. All of the figures represent specific people, divided into two camps – speculative thinkers on the left with Plato, and fact-seekers on the right supporting Aristotle. Plato is said to be a portrait of Leonardo, while Heraclitus (rather glumly seated, and resting his head on his hand) is a tribute to Michelangelo.

△ **The Miraculous Draught of Fishes** 1515-16
Raphael (1483-1520)

Watercolours on paper

IN 1515 RAPHAEL was commissioned by Pope Leo X to provide cartoons (preliminary designs or guides) for a set of ten tapestries, to be woven in Flanders, for the lower walls of the Sistine Chapel. This meant they had to stand comparison with Michelangelo's mighty painted ceiling as well as with frescoes by Perugino, Botticelli and Ghirlandaio. Raphael rose to the challenge, creating large, imposing figures who dominate the picture area, and treating the biblical scenes with a new sense of dramatic intensity. *The Miraculous Draught of Fishes* is based on a New Testament episode in which Jesus summoned Simon Peter, James and John to be his disciples. Having made a miraculously large catch, the impulsive Simon Peter fell to his knees, crying 'Depart from me; for I am a sinful man, O Lord.' But Jesus told him that from now on he and his partners would be 'fishers of men'. Used as the basis for further sets of tapestries, and widely reproduced as engravings, the cartoons were among Raphael's most influential works.

△ The Tempest c.1500
Giorgione (c.1478-1510)

Canvas

GIORGIONE transformed Venetian painting, but his life is very poorly documented and only a handful of paintings can be attributed to him with any certainty. In the most celebrated of these, *The Tempest*, Giorgione introduced a new genre, dispensing with a definable subject and creating the 'mood' painting in which poetic resonance matters more than the 'programme'. The human figures are not involved with one another, but are caught up in the heavy atmosphere of a summer day about to be overwhelmed by the storm; thunder clouds and lightning are visible in the distance over the town. The broken columns and overgrown ruins add another ominous note; they have since had a long history as melancholy symbols of transience. Although *The Tempest* is not a landscape painting, it was as close to pure landscape as the Renaissance ever came, anticipating a genre not fully established until the 17th century.

△ The Madonna of the Harpies 1517
Andrea del Sarto (1486-1530)

Panel

BY ABOUT 1508 ROME had replaced Florence as the artistic capital of Italy. Florence nonetheless continued to produce painters of great ability, among whom Andrea del Sarto occupied a commanding position. His *Madonna of the Harpies* is as much a work of the High Renaissance as anything produced in Rome – large and grand, with idealized figures, restrained emotion and a composition which gives the painting its stable, durable air. The Virgin and Child are enthroned, with St Francis of Assisi and St John the Evangelist in attendance; it is not clear why del Sarto included harpies round the plinth. The tinge of gentle melancholy in the picture is characteristic of his work.

△ **Concert Champêtre** c.1510
Giorgione (c.1478-1510) or Titian (c.1487-1576)

Canvas

DESPITE CENTURIES of debate, no verdict has been reached on the authorship of this wonderful picture. It may have been painted by Giorgione shortly before he was carried off by the plague, or finished by Titian, his fellow-Venetian, after Giorgione's death; or it may be an early masterpiece by Titian himself. Critical opinion has fluctuated over the years, recently favouring Titian's sole authorship. However, the case for Giorgione remains strong, if only because, unlike the young Titian, he had already reached artistic maturity. The soft, warm flesh of the women

and the silky, colourful fabrics make this an exquisitely sensual and sensuous painting; but the general mood is gentle and idyllic. As in *The Tempest*, the figures are not set against a landscape background, but are part of the scene – though we can hardly doubt that these are urban sophisticates, intent on enjoying country pleasures withheld from the rather glum-looking shepherd. With or without music-making, the *fête champêtre*, picturing elegant people in a landscape, became one of the most delightful traditions of European art.

△ **The Assumption of the Virgin** c.1518
Titian (c.1487-1576)

Canvas

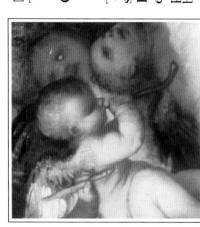

Detail

TITIAN BECAME the most sought-after painter in Europe, and enjoyed an extraordinarily long and prosperous career. His date of birth is not known, and it used to be believed that he was born in about 1477 and lived to be almost 100. Nowadays this is thought unlikely, though not impossible. Titian's early years were spent in the shadow of Giorgione (pages 62-5), and until 1510 it is sometimes difficult to distinguish between the works of the two artists. Titian's first documented paintings were frescoes

executed in Padua. In 1516 the aged Giovanni Bellini died and Titian became the official painter to the Venetian state. *The Assumption of the Virgin* was his first great public commission in Venice. The subject had previously been treated rather quietly, and so Titian's dramatic intensity and sumptuous colours made a tremendous impact. Though Giorgione's lyricism remained an influence on him, Titian now emerged as the master of a distinctly monumental, colourful and energetic style.

△ **The Venus of Urbino** 1538
Titian (c. 1487-1576)

Canvas

TITIAN UNDOUBTEDLY painted this with a much earlier but broadly similar painting by Giorgione, *The Sleeping Venus*, in mind. The fact that he did so, almost 30 years after Giorgione's death, suggests that Titian still felt a sense of rivalry with the master who had dominated Venetian painting in his youth. Where Giorgione's untroubled Venus lies sleeping in a landscape, Titian's more sophisticated goddess is fully conscious of the spectator, whose viewpoint might be that of a lover entering her room. There is perhaps no more

captivating, dewy, inviting nude in the history of European painting. But there is nothing gross about her sensuality, although some Victorians felt otherwise – notably Mark Twain, whose famous sense of humour deserted him in front of the picture, which he denounced with all the frenzy of lust repressed. Over the centuries, the pose and setting of *The Venus of Urbino* were widely imitated and adapted, not least by the French Impressionist Edouard Manet for his famous and scandalously 'modern' *Olympia*.

△ Diana Surprised by Actaeon c.1558
Titian (c.1487-1576)

Canvas

IN 1533 CHARLES V bestowed on Titian the title of Count Palatine, an unprecedented honour for an artist. Charles's son, Philip II of Spain, patronized Titian even more lavishly than his father had done, ordering a series of mythological scenes in which the erotic interest was remarkably thinly disguised. However, whether he realized it or not, he was also acquiring some of the master's finest works, painted at the very height of his powers. As he moved into old age, Titian's brushwork became increasingly free and his colours ever richer. *Diana Surprised by Actaeon* pictures the moment when Actaeon, a young hunter, chanced upon the goddess Diana and her attendant nymphs while they were bathing. The tragic outcome (a furious Diana changed Actaeon into a stag and he was torn to pieces by his own hounds) is hardly hinted at in this painting of dazzling colours, textures and light effects.

△ Pope Paul III and his Nephews 1546
Titian (c.1487-1576)

Canvas

ASTONISHINGLY PROLIFIC, Titian became pre-eminent as a painter of religious and mythological subjects, and also as a portraitist. Every one of his sitters comes over to us as a distinct personality, ranging from poets and boors to the wizened Pope Paul III and his *nipoti. Nipoti* is the Italian word for 'nephews' – and also for 'grandchildren', which is what these two rather shifty-looking characters actually were. The 'nephews' were Ottavio Farnese, shown stooping in order to listen to his grandfather, and Cardinal Alessandro Farnese, the only member of the group who seems to be self-consciously posing for his portrait. The tense atmosphere of the painting accurately reflects the reality of Farnese family intrigues.

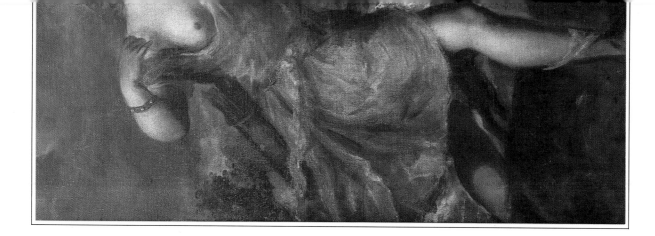

△ **The Death of Actaeon** c. 1562
Titian (c. 1487-1576)

Canvas

TITIAN WAS THE FIRST great European artist to take many of his subjects from classical mythology, encouraged by regular commissions from King Philip II of Spain. The king's interest was not exclusively artistic, for the chosen subjects were often highly erotic, especially when executed with Titian's mastery of flesh tones and textures. However, in *The Death of Actaeon* the mood is darker. A few years earlier Titian had painted the scene in which Actaeon, a young hunter, chanced upon the goddess Diana and her attendant nymphs while they were bathing. Here he pays the price for his unintended sacrilege. The goddess has changed him into a stag and he is being brought down by his own hounds, while Diana herself takes part in the chase. The picture is a striking product of Titian's old age, still full of energy and richness; and the growing European interest in landscape is also apparent in the prominence give to the wooded background.

△ Moses striking Water from the Rock 1577
Tintoretto (1518-94)

Canvas

Detail

KNOWN AS TINTORETTO because he was the son of a dyer, Jacopo Robusti seems to have been an individual as frenziedly energetic as the scenes in his paintings. Driven by vanity, piety and love of art to grasp at every available commission and create on a vast scale, he was a fast worker in both senses of the words. On one notorious occasion, when tenders were invited for a ceiling painting, his rivals turned up with drawings and models, only to find that in the meantime Tintoretto had sneaked into the building and completed the picture on the spot! Appropriately, this piece of one-upmanship was perpetrated in the Scuola di San Rocco, the headquarters of a Venetian charitable society which eventually became a treasure-house of over 50 Tintorettos. *Moses striking Water from the Rock* displays his dramatic energy, his use of large agitated groups of people, his thrusting compositions, and the effect of mystic intensity he was able to convey with explosions of bright light against dark backgrounds.

△ **The Marriage Feast at Cana** 1564
Paolo Veronese (c.1528-1588)

Fresco

PAOLO CALIARI WAS BORN and trained in Verona (hence his nickname) before coming to Venice in 1553 to work on the Doge's palace. Veronese is celebrated for his large-scale banqueting scenes, often nominally on religious subjects. At Cana, Jesus performed his first miracle, turning jars of water into wine so that the marriage feast could go on. Typically, Veronese uses the occasion to portray the Venetian lifestyle at its most luxurious, with confident, sumptuously costumed diners and their retinue. The grand setting and the throng of diners and bystanders make it easy to overlook Jesus and Mary altogether, although the steward's critical examination of the wine commands our attention. Yet Veronese's materialism is so large, colourful and straightforward that it finally wins most of us over.

▷ **Jupiter and Io** c.1532
Correggio (1494–1534)

Canvas

ANTONIO ALLEGRI was nicknamed Correggio, after his birthplace in the Romagna. He mainly worked in the nearest large town, Parma, developing a style which owed something to the amplitude of the High Renaissance but was in most respects a personal creation, more agitated and emotional. A painter of soft, melting surfaces and charming figures, he introduced an erotic note into much of his work, even when its subjects were purportedly religious. *Jupiter and Io* is a direct transcription of the classical myth in which the king of the gods disguised himself as a cloud in order to have his way with the daughter of the king of Argos. The god's materialized paw and dimly discernable features, and above all the smile on the lady's face, made this a daringly explicit scene in its day; and Correggio's lovely light and sensuous effects are still a delight.

▽ **The Madonna with the Long Neck** 1534-40
Parmigianino (1503-40)

Panel

BORN IN PARMA, and consequently known as Il Parmigianino, Francesco Mazzola was one of the earliest of the artists who have since been labelled Mannerists; they reacted to the dead-end perfection of the High Renaissance by developing or over-developing some aspect of it, undermining its classical calm and balance. Parmigianino delighted in a rather perverse beauty and elegant distortion. His ultra-refinement culminated in the elongated figures of this painting, commissioned in 1534 but never finished; since the very effective phallic column was supposed to be a colonnade, the artist may have sensed that this Madonna was best left 'unfinished'. Apart from the Madonna's long fingers and neck (emphasized by her sloping shoulders), her baby is a giant who, if placed upright, would not be so very much shorter than the manly maids or maidenly young men crowding round the couple.

ACKNOWLEDGEMENTS

The publisher would like to thank the following for their kind permission to reproduce the paintings in this book:

Bridgeman Art Library, London/Scrovegni, (Arena) Chapel,Padua: 8; /Galleria degli Uffizi, Florence: 9; /Baptistry, Florence Cathedral/Giraudon: 10-11; /Brancacci Chapel, Santa Maria del Carmine, Florence: 12-13, 14; /Galleria degli Uffizi, Florence: 15, 16; /Museo di San Marco dell'Angelico, Florence: 17; /Galleria degli Uffizi, Florence: 19; /Galleria Nazionale delle Marche, Urbino: 20; /Pinacoteca di Brera, Milan: 21; /Palazzo Medici-Riccardi, Florence: 22-23; /National Gallery, London: 24, 24-25, 26; /Pinacoteca di Brera, Milan: 27; /Palazzo Ducale, Mantua: 29; /National Gallery, London: 30; /Galleria degli Uffizi, Florence: 31; /Galleria degli Uffizi: 32-33, 34-35; /Vatican Museums & Galleries, Rome: 36-37; /Louvre, Paris: 38; /Piccolomini Library, Siena Cathedral/Photo: F. Lensini, Siena: 39; /Galleria dell' Accademia, Venice: 40; /National Gallery, London: 42-43; /Czartorisky Museum, Cracow: 44; /Santa Maria della Grazie, Milan: 45; /Louvre, Paris/Giraudon: 46; /National Gallery, London: 47; /St Peter's, Vatican: 48; /Galleria dell'Accademia, Florence: 49; /Galleria degli Uffizi, Florence: 51; /Vatican Museums & Galleries, Rome: 54-55, 56-57, Cover, Half-title; /Louvre, Paris /Giraudon: 59; /Victoria & Albert Museum, London: 60-61; /Galleria degli Uffizi, Florence: 62; /Galleria dell'Accademia, Venice: 63; /Louvre, Paris/Giraudon: 64-65; /Santa Maria dei Frari, Venice/Photo: Francesco Turio Bohm: 67; /Galleria degli Uffizi, Florence: 68-69; /Museo & Gallerie Nazionale di Capodimonte, Naples: 70; /Duke of Sutherland Collection, National Gallery of Scotland, Edinburgh: 71; /National Gallery, London: 72-73; /Scuola Grande di San Rocco, Venice: 75; /Louvre, Paris: 76; /Kunsthistorisches Museum, Vienna: 77; /Galleria degli Uffizi, Florence: 78

© **Nippon Television Network Corporation, Tokyo, 1995:** 52-53

Every effort has been made to trace the copyright holders and we apologise in advance for any unintentional omissions. We would be pleased to insert the appropriate acknowledgement in any subsequent edition of this publication.